OLYMPUSVILLE

OLYMPUSVILLE

poems by
RON KOERTGE

with illustrations by
ALICIA KLEMAN

Red Hen Press | Pasadena, CA

Illustrations by Alicia Kleman
Book design by Selena Trager

Library of Congress Cataloging-in-Publication Data
Names: Koertge, Ronald, author.
Title: Olympusville / by Ron Koertge.
Description: Pasadena, California: Red Hen Press, [2018]
Identifiers: LCCN 2017051907 | ISBN 9781597091084 (softcover) |
    eISBN 9781597096959
Subjects: LCSH: Mythology, Greek—Poetry.
Classification: LCC PS3561.O347 A6 2018 | DDC 811/.54—dc23
LC record available at https://lccn.loc.gov/2017051907

The National Endowment for the Arts, the Los Angeles County Arts Commission,
the Ahmanson Foundation, the Dwight Stuart Youth Fund, the Max Factor Family
Foundation, the Pasadena Tournament of Roses Foundation, the Pasadena Arts &
Culture Commission and the City of Pasadena Cultural Affairs Division, the City
of Los Angeles Department of Cultural Affairs, the Audrey & Sydney Irmas Char-
itable Foundation, the Kinder Morgan Foundation, the Allergan Foundation, the
Riordan Foundation, and the Amazon Literary Partnership partially support Red
Hen Press.

First Edition
Red Hen Press
www.redhen.org

.

Where you are in the world now it is dark.
—JO McDOUGALL
"Walking Down Prospect"

The world hikes up her skirts and her
underthings are so lovely!
—AMY GERSTLER
"Debris Trail"

CONTENTS

OLYMPUSVILLE

SISYPHUS

Don't get me started on the gods. What a bunch of windbags. *It's too wet under the sea. I limp and my wife cheats on me. My husband sees other women. My father devoured me.* It never ends. Immortal and unsatisfied. I'm at least interesting. I told Zeus to go to Hell, but he sent me there instead. Did I moan and groan? No—I tricked Death into the chains meant for me. He's such a dim bulb! And while I had him under lock and key, nobody died. Stasis ruled. I made that happen. *I ruled.* Me, the poor bastard with the boulder. Symbol of futility. Avatar of office drones with Sisyphus cartoons pinned to the cubicle walls. I pity them because they don't accept their fate. Much less relish it. Things are so preposterous it's almost farcical. That there's a world at all. That gods exist or care. That life isn't fair. That someone loves you. Every day I climb and every day the boulder descends. As I walk down to begin again, I breathe deeply and look around. I have to laugh. You should hear the damned go on and on about their sins. You should see Persephone prancing around teasing Tantalus, and I even make Narcissus look up from his little mirror. You know what their problem is? Hope. I don't bother with that. I have my beloved boulder which I lean on as we begin again our journey up. My world is small but it is my world.

When other little boys were writing things in the sand with sticks, I was turning sand into glass with thunderbolts. I'm King of the Gods. Not just a god. King of all the gods. Of everything. I'm wise. I'm powerful. I'm irresistible. Did you know I can change myself into an ant and still seduce anybody in five minutes flat? Women adore me. Ask Leda. Ask Io and Themis. Ask Mnemosyne. Her nine daughters from our nine wonderful nights together are the Muses. Without them—without me!—there's no poetry or history or dance or astronomy. Speaking of nine, King Pierus said his daughters were as beautiful and talented as my daughters. *My* muses. What was he thinking? Thanks to his insolence, instead of daughters he has nine chattering magpies. I am the keeper of oaths, patron of the marketplace and of hospitality, avenger of wrongs done to strangers. I'm worshipped in Antioch and Crete and Athens. But I'll tell you a little secret: when I can't sleep I don't think about reverence or acclaim. I don't think about vengeance or retribution, much less white thighs in the moonlight or breasts garnished with honey. I think about the past. As a baby I was spirited away to Crete. Nymphs raised me on the milk of a goat named Amaltheia. I played in the sun and wrestled with wolf cubs. I loved the sound of everything. Now all I hear are by-the-numbers prayers and petty complaints. And then there's Hera, my wife, who never shuts up.

ZEUS

My brothers are Zeus and Poseidon. When we beat the Titans, the world was ours, so we gambled for it. I got the dark world, Poseidon the wet one. Zeus was lucky, as usual. Not only is he the sky god, he has beautiful Hera, and he cheats on her night and day. I would never do that. I was so lonely in the dark surrounded by the dead that one day I wrapped my sooty hand around Persephone's alabaster ankle and brought her home. My home. She was bored to death shopping and arranging flowers. And I deserve a beautiful wife. Someone by my side. Someone who loves me. And Persephone does love me. She's a queen now, and not just a silly girl under her mother's thumb. She grew up fast. She insists we make love every night, even if I don't feel like it. I don't mind. I like to make every moment count since I get to see her, be with her, hold her only half a year. Thanks to Zeus. To shut up a mother who would let the world die just to see her daughter in a new yellow dress. In my realm is a Chair of Forgetfulness. It's punishment for anyone who tries to take one of my guests. But when Persephone leaves me for six months, I want to sit in it and forget how rich I am, how powerful I am, how I rule over a million souls. And then six months later I see her coming, smelling like that other world and I forget everything but her.

HADES

APHRODITE

I can't keep my clothes on. And why should I? I'm Beauty and Pleasure, not Blemish and Melancholy. I have a husband, Hephaestus, but his mother threw him away. How can I take someone like that seriously? He's God of the Forge but half the people I know are gods. He gives me things he made but they're bribes. If they could talk they'd say *Love me Love me Love me*. Ares doesn't talk much. He comes to me straight from some war. There I am in that little blue pleated skirt he likes and we hop right into bed. We were never exactly discreet and once we got caught red-handed. When Helios was about to drive his sun chariot across the sky, Ares kissed me one last time. But that kiss led to, well, other things. We didn't know Hephaestus was onto us. We certainly didn't know he'd made a beautiful golden mesh to trap us when we finally got out of bed. But he had and we were. He called the other gods as witnesses to our folly, but we weren't ashamed. When they all saw me naked and content, they couldn't look away. They didn't want to judge me. Instead they made fun of Hephaestus who saw what a fool he'd made of himself. Then Ares left like he always does. If Adonis is with Persephone, I feel so alone! So when my husband comes in hot from the forge, soot-covered and chagrined, I hide his ugly legs in the huge golden bath he made for me. I concentrate on his powerful shoulders and chest. This is how I pretend to love him and in a way I do.

ARES

Let's see: extermination, slaughter, assassination, liquidation, genocide, or carnage. I check All of the Above. Here's how I go to war: win it and move on, leaving the bodies behind. My sister Athena: it's chess to her. Strategy. I don't have time to stand over a table and move toys around on a map. I wade in and leave bloody footsteps. My children follow me: Terror, Fear, Discord. One big happy family. Zeus is my father and he hates me because I'm bloodthirsty. I'd kill him if I could, the hypocritical bastard. He does anything he wants with anybody he wants. I win battles. Anybody else would be a hero, but according to him, I'm a warmonger and a brute. He flits from woman to woman, breaking my mother's heart. He's a rapist in a swan suit and nobody says a word. He's a swan, an eagle, a bull, a freaking ant! Anything to get their clothes off. And there I am more or less faithful to Aphrodite who's married to that cripple Hephaestus. If she would let me, I would kill him. But who can get her attention when she's fighting with Persephone over that useless pretty boy Adonis. Still, when I don't have a sword in my hands, all I want to do is lie in Aphrodite's arms with my faithful dog beside me. In the air above us—vultures.

I don't need to borrow a mirror from Narcissus. I was such a beautiful baby that Aphrodite couldn't think of anything or anybody else. When she needed a sitter she handed me over to Persephone. It was love at first sight. She was Queen of the Underworld. She carried me through Hades, and the ghosts fought to touch me because I was like cool water. Persephone and I spent every minute together. We'd go see Cerberus who let me pet him. We'd drop in on Grief, Anxicty, and Disease. For me they were doting aunties with toys and snacks. I'd fall asleep and the damned would stop howling till I woke up. Hades was jealous, but Persephone had him wrapped around her finger. She let him make love to her every night, then while he was crashed out she'd come into my room and we'd draw or sing songs. She'd call me glitter bug and buttercup, angel puss and sweet cakes. Then I grew up and Aphrodite wanted me back. That's when the trouble started. Persephone said, "No way." Aphrodite threatened her. Persephone said that she'd have her

ADONIS

husband send ghosts to haunt her. Aphrodite said that she was a goddess and nobody threatens a goddess. Finally Zeus stepped in—three months with Aphrodite, then three months with Persephone. That got old fast, shuttling from one to the other. Where was I supposed to keep my good clothes? Anyway, it was more fun to be with Aphrodite. She was nearly as beautiful as I. Wherever we went people bought us drinks and paid for our dinner. Things were going great until I was attacked by a boar, the ugliest animal in the world. That was bad enough but I'm also pretty sure it was really shape-shifting Ares who hated anyone that Aphrodite even talked to, the jealous fool.

HEPHAESTUS

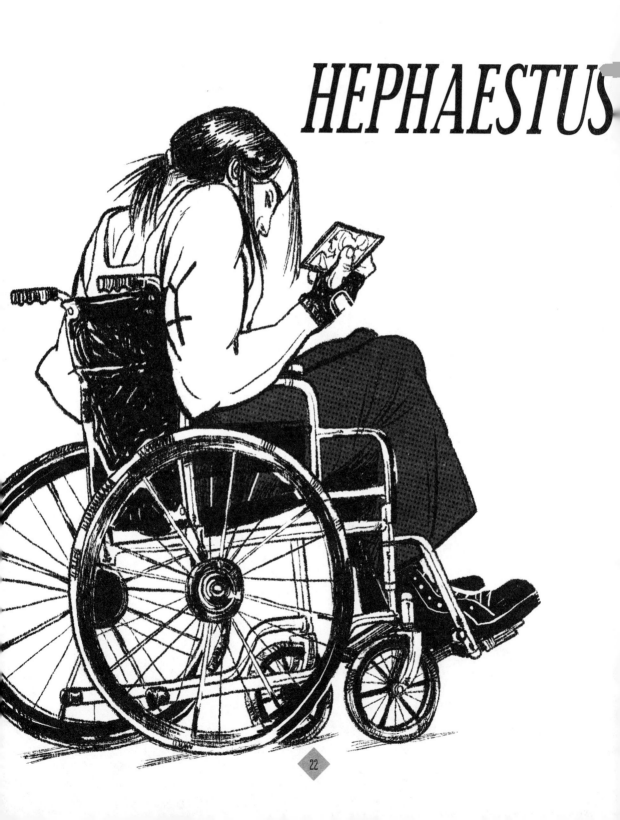

im so ugly my mom threw me down a mountain way down i
ended up on an eyeland and got taut how to do stuff with my hands
i was pretty good so my dad wanted me back on the mounton to
make things and i did i made shields and war stuff i did a belt for
my wife and when she wore it everybody went nuts for her she
fooled around a lot anyway cause she didnt want to marry me in
the first place and some nymphs i knew said catch her atit catch
heratit so i made a net outta real fine gold and caught her and this
ares guy and there they were naked and o man she looked great
like that and he did to he was everything im not so yeah i just
slunk away wile everybody laffed at me but what i was thinking
also you no what theres nobody could make a net like that but me
in my workshop i made gold things that walked around and gold
dogs that barked i made a chariot for the sky god to ride across
the sky in or itd be dark all the time did you hear about the gold
throne for my mom when she sat in it she couldnt get up ha ha i
showed her and then we kinda made up i have girlfriends cause
you know i live on ohlimpus and my dad is zeus it isnt my looks
thats for sure but im strong a lot and some girls like that looks
arent so important to everybody thank god im a god cause im not
that good with people if i make a mistake making a gold thing i
just tell the gold im sorry and bend it back or melt it down i cant
do that with aphrodite she dont bend like that bow i made for
artemis now aphrodites not sorry for a thing she does and i
admire that but guys I work with say make yurself a girl outta gold
that walks and talks and who will do any old thing but i say no
cause im married for one thing and for another   ok i dont
know the other but i just dont want to do it i guess im not sure
why.

Here's what Hesiod says about me: ". . . delighting in arrows, lovely in shape like none of the gods." Hesiod exaggerates. Aphrodite is more beautiful than I. Even a mortal like Semele has more allure. But beauty to many women is a burden: *Will it fade? Will anyone ever see the real me? What does it mean when my husband is late for dinner again?* I didn't want any part of that. My father is Zeus. When I was little I sat on his lap and asked 1. to always be a virgin, 2. to have a beautiful bow and arrows, 3. to have twenty nymphs to serve me. Everyone knows how fathers can be about daughters: I got everything I asked for. So while some foolish goddesses obsess about their husbands or lovers, I am faithful to myself and happy with my companions and the forests. It sounds sylvan, doesn't it. Women alone bathing at will, whispering, napping when we're tired, eating together, drifting from glen to valley to pool to waterfall. And it is sylvan and sensual. But it isn't all fun and games. My dear friend Orion died because someone I trusted lied to me. When Niobe disrespected me, my brother and I killed her fourteen children. I changed Callisto into a bear though she deserved worse for what she'd done. When Actæon saw me naked, I was too bright for him to rest his eyes on. I turned him into a stag. My nymphs and I watched his hounds rip him to pieces. The list of my dark accomplishments goes

ARTEMIS

on and on. I am not to be trifled with by small men. No one scorns me or my companions. I am not just a girl who likes to run around in the woods with her little bow and arrows.

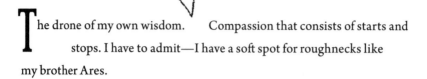

The drone of my own wisdom.   Compassion that consists of starts and
        stops. I have to admit—I have a soft spot for roughnecks like
my brother Ares.

                        The river is kin to the shore, which is first cousin
to the trees that feather-dust the sky where I live and humans pray to me
        through a big, bolted door.

        I spend hours away from Olympus. Hours away from my temples.
I like to wander and feel the human love-pull.

        I listen in on the other world.
The clink of silverware, the dark slurp of coffee on real lips.

        Elaborate prayers can make my skin crawl.
                But let someone ask for bread and milk and before they
can open their eyes there it is.

                I attend funerals and stand in the back. Everyone's lost
someone. I'm not so different.
                I have a golden comb and a nymph to untangle the snarls in my
hair but the tears are the same.

        I would save a mouse in the snow
yet when Arachne wove scenes of Leda and my father, her with a hand
around the thick neck,

                        a look of ecstasy on her face, I shamed her and
turned her into a spider. They forget I was born fully grown, sheathed in
armor. With a taste for birdsong and the colder medium of battle.

I'm a lot of things.
Mostly fair but tough.

If I wanted to
I could be hot stuff.

ATHENA

GYM →

DEMETER

I should have known. Boys started sniffing around my daughter like jackals. The same thing happened to me years ago (a few years ago) but I was (and am) a goddess and immensely wise. Persephone, beautiful as she is (or was!) with skin that would light up the darkest alley, is also naïve. I'm fertility, I'm fecundity. She's not and never will be. Of course I didn't want her stolen, abducted, snatched, made off with, spirited away. And where did she go? Even her father wouldn't tell me. He was too busy raping someone else's daughters. So I took a hostage: Earth itself. I cursed it till it was barren, sterile, dead, and everybody starved while I looked for her. You should have heard the pleas. The prayers. The petitions and supplications. I refused to hear a word while I searched far and wide. I broke a nail! I got a callus! Where were the nymphs who used to rub my feet with warm oil? Finally Helios, the sun god, told me where Persephone was. Hades. Of all places. I got to picture his sooty hands on her. I could almost taste his anthracite breath. It was too much to bear. I finally tracked down Zeus when he had his pants on and we struck a bargain. Six months with Hades, six with me. But my daughter is different now. Slightly distant. Almost smug. She says it's because she's a married woman, but I say that I am, too. Shouldn't that bring us closer? She just looks the other way and plays with her hair like a three-year-old! If I break down and ask her if anything's wrong she says the four words that pierce my heart. "Mom, I miss Hades." Is it true or does she say it just to torture me?

I'm famous for being abducted. Famous for being my mother's lost child. Famous for being the wife of Hades. I'm like those kids with different weekends for different parents, except I stay for six months at a time. If I forget my good shoes, I can't go back! What a drag. My famous husband smells like smoke. All his friends are phantoms and wraiths. Imagine a crowd sitting around in your living room drinking and playing cards night after night. Doesn't that sound romantic? I was a dumb bunny picking flowers when he came at me. Do you know what he said afterward from his bedroom in Hell, "But you're a queen now. What were you before except a silly girl. Have another diamond. You'll feel better." Thank Zeus I'm away from him for six months. Spring and summer. The trouble is in the other world cute boys won't have anything to do with me. And what are my girlfriends supposed to say to their kids, "Oh, look. It's my old friend Persephone. Maybe some of the dead she rules over will come to lunch, too. Wouldn't that be nice?" No wonder I think of Adonis all the time. Aphrodite gave him to me for a little while when he was barely more than a baby saying she would come for him later. Like he was something on a lay-away plan. His beauty was astonishing. I fell in love with him. Not like Hades is in love with me only at night after I've taken a bath. Holding Adonis remapped my brain. Something inside me unfurled. Me times him = more than I thought I'd ever know. When he died, Aphrodite flew to him. At the time, I was under my husband who was ordering me to moan louder so everyone in Hell would know what a great lover he was. Six months in hell every year. Then six with my mother. And Adonis only a memory.

PERSEPHONE

HERA

Zeus is a rock star. I don't expect a husband like that to act like some browbeaten schmuck from Piddleyville. He comes home to me. His wife. That's what counts. Every year I turn into a virgin again. Can any of the others say that? Callisto or Ganymede or Io or Semele? Speaking of Semele, she was the fool who wanted to see my husband in all his glory. Any mortal would have turned to soot. And Io had hips like a heifer before I turned her into one, so her life wasn't all that different. What did any of my husband's tootsies have besides their novelty. They were passing fancies at best. Whims. Everyone knows the Milky Way. How many lovers have lain sated in sweet grass and marveled at the hundred billion stars. Well, that is my milk up there spewed across the heavens from breasts that drive Zeus mad with desire. Can Nemesis top that? Or Mnemosyne? And let's be clear about that one and her so-called beautiful hair. I told Zeus to sleep with her once because in my wisdom I knew she would be the mother of a muse. I admit I didn't think he'd stay a week and a half, but now we have Nine Muses thanks to me and they all celebrate me in poetry and dance and song. And for the record, in the beginning Zeus ran after me, not the other way around. I knew his reputation, but when he showed up as a poor little bird and I cradled him and he turned into himself in all his glory and there was his Zeus-ness . . . well. I said yes. And let's never forget—when we went on our honeymoon, it lasted three hundred years! Let Echo, that little traitor, repeat that!

I wasted away, so now I can say anything and not just what someone else said *what someone else said else said*. Oh, it lingers, doesn't it? I'm in Hades, one of his guests. I'd like to tell him how often Persephone thinks about Adonis but I'm afraid *afraid afraid*. I don't deserve to be down here! All I did was serve Zeus, King of the Gods, when he came to the mountains to do you-know-what with almost anybody. He might have really loved me *loved me me me*, but then I would have been like all the other girls he "really loved." Instead, I kept Hera busy. I admit it was kind of pimpy, but Zeus pleaded with me instead of just doing you-know-what then vanishing. I thought too much of myself for his kind of monkey business even if he was Zeus. So while he did, you know, with whoever, I'd chat with Hera and keep her busy. Tell her how beautiful she was, how lucky in love *love love*. It worked until it didn't. She was so mad! Since when does a goddess even know those words! No wonder Zeus fooled around. Can you imagine coming home to that every night *every night*? I'm lucky she didn't kill me. The other nymphs hid me until I fell for Narcissus. Isn't love strange? He didn't know I was alive! But it didn't matter. I loved him, anyway. One of the last things he said as he gazed into his pool was, "Farewell." It tolled like

ECHO

a bell. Even if he wasn't talking to me, I repeated it as I grew
less and less a girl, then less than that, then just a whisper on
the air *on the air the air.*

Me me me me me me me me me me me me me
me me me me me me me me me me me me me
me me me me me me me me me me me me me
me me me me me me me me me me me me me
me me me me me me me me me me me me me
me me me me me me me me me me me me me
me me me me me me me me me me me me me
me me me me me me me me me me me me me
me me me me me me me me me me me me me
me me me me me me me me me me me me me
me me me   me me me
me me me   me me me
me me   me me
me me   my picture here   me me
me me me   me me me
me me me   me me me
me me me   me me me
me me me me me me me me me me me me
me me me me me me me me me me me me
me me me me me me me me me me me me
me me me me me me me me me me me me
me me me me me me me me me me me me
me me me me me me me me me me me me
me me me me me me me me me me me me
me me me me me me me me me me me me
me me me me me me me me me me me me
me me me me me me me me me me me me
me me me me me me me me me me me me
me me me me me me me me me me me me
me me me me me me me me me me me me
me me me me me me me me me me me me

NARCISSUS

I know what everyone thinks: I live on the ocean floor. I use my trident to cause earthquakes. I'm moody and hard to handle. All true. And old news. No one ever talks about how I have deep feelings. Like how I felt about Caenis, a nymph I was in love with. Yes. Not just lust, like my brother Zeus, that immortal fraternity boy. Once after Caenis and I had made love I was so happy that I promised her anything and you'll never guess. She

didn't want a palace or a mountain of gold. She wanted to be a man. And not any man but a warrior that no weapon could kill. I keep my promises but this time with such a heavy heart. Reluctantly, I waved my hand and there he stood with a new name (Caeneus), helmet and spear, and the rest of the apparatus that makes a man a man. I can't describe the grief I felt. The sense of loss. Yet he was elated, thanking me profusely, saying that except when I touched her she was restless in her womanhood, counterfeit in a way. But now genuine at last. He embraced me like a brother. I knew it might end badly. He was a great warrior and one day when his blood was up he rashly ordered everyone to worship his spear as a god. When I heard this, my heart sank. I knew Zeus would find a way to punish him. And did. As Caeneus died, suffocated by drunken centaurs, he turned back into Caenis. One last glimpse of the woman I'd loved before I killed every one of those half-horse–half-man monstrosities. Then I dove into the sea to wash the blood away.

POSEIDON

NYMPHS

We're water nymphs or mountain nymphs: Naiads and Oreads. Everybody knows we love groves, pastures, trees, glens, springs, lakes. But the names we call each other, names that are warm in the mouth, are secret. We can live a long time, but trees die, wells dry up. Does anyone besides her sisters mourn the passing of a nymph? Our version of happiness is each other and the natural world. It doesn't really include babysitting. But Artemis asked Daddy for handmaidens and Zeus recruited us, dimming his glory so we could see him and not end up like poor Semele who just went poof! Everyone knows how Zeus is and we thought he was here for that, so which one of us would he choose? I looked right back at him and he laughed. Zeus likes sass. He touched my shoulder. His breath in my ear was like an aria. "Take care of my daughter," he said. So we protect Artemis, listen for the rustle in the underbrush, the panting of some hunter's hounds, his laser eyes. Between ourselves we whisper, *It's just another stupid man*. We confound those every day. But we gather around her, make a fence for her nakedness even though we're mostly-naked, voluptuous and shadowy and dripping wet, too. Usually they die like that Actæon guy. But sometimes they get away. Imagine the stories they tell if they find their way home. There are twenty of us, like a small sorority. We fall in and out of love with each other all the time but we keep that away from Artemis. We're essentially her slaves. Yes, ma'am. No, ma'am. Can we bring you anything? Would you like to take a nap? We love it when she's asleep. Then we can be, for a little while, our true selves.

BIOGRAPHICAL NOTE

A prolific writer, Ron Koertge was published widely in the '60s and '70s in such seminal magazines as *Kayak* and *Poetry Now*. His first book, *The Father Poems*, was published in 1973, and was soon followed by many more, including poetry, prose, novels-in-verse, and fiction for teenagers. His most recent book, *Vampire Planet*, was released in 2016 from Red Hen Press. Ron is the recipient of grants from the NEA and the California Arts Council, has poems in two volumes of *Best American Poetry* (1999 and 2005), and is a 2017 Pushcart Prize winner. His fiction has been honored by the American Library Association, and two novels have received PEN awards. After teaching for thirty-seven years at the city college in Pasadena, he retired and now teaches at Hamline University in their low-residency MFA program for Children's Writing. He currently lives in South Pasadena, California, with his wife, Bianca Richards.